BLARIS MOOR

MEDBH

MCGUCKIAN

WAKE FOREST UNIVERSITY PRESS

BLARIS

MOOR

WINSTON-SALEM, NORTH CAROLINA

First North American edition
© Medbh McGuckian, 2016
Edited by Peter Fallon and first published by
The Gallery Press in Ireland in 2015
All rights reserved. No part of this book
may be reproduced in any form without prior
permission in writing from the publishers.
For permission, write to
Wake Forest University Press
Post Office Box 7333
Winston-Salem, NC 27109
wfupress.wfu.edu
wfupress@wfu.edu
ISBN 978-1-930630-78-9 (paperback)
Library of Congress Control Number 2016938997
Designed and typeset by Quemadura
Publication of this book was generously
supported by the Boyle Family Fund.

CONTENTS

An Early Apocalypse 1

The Reading Fever 2

The Nymph Hay 3

The Stone-word 4

Trans-shipment Station 5

Musk 6

Animals of the Mind 8

The Contents of the Cupboard 11

Tavoletta 15

The Rainbow Division 17

How Despair May Be Transformed into a Diamond 21

The Migration of the Nobles, 1603 22

By the Entrails of Christ 24

Virginia Will Become Aughanure 25

Primrose Red Orchestra 26

Santo Spirito Lands on Mars 28

White Cortina Outside Stardust Ballroom 30

The Statement of My Right Honourable Friend 32

The Questioning of Soldier L 35

Note for Blind Therapists 37

A Novel About Patrick 40

Reading Before Stalin 43

Verses Unpublished in the Poet's Lifetime
WORKS AND DAYS 44

OUR DAYS 44

ABOUT THAT 44

SEASONAL MOOD PICTURE 45

SKETCHES FOR A FANTASY 45

POEM OF A KINSMAN 45

SYMPATHY FOR THE TWILIGHT 46

MUSE OF CINEMA 46

THE BLACK GOBLET 46

DREAM OF A FIRST LOVE'S MARRIAGE 47

REVENGE AGAINST MUSIC 47

YOUR DEATH 47

SYNAGOGUE WEDDING 48

RED CORNFIELD 48

RAIN-SPANGLED POEM 48

TO THE DEMON'S MEMORY 49

THE COURTYARD 49

LYRE OF LYRES 49

OCTOBER'S MAN OF THE MOMENT 50

UNEXTINGUISHED MOON 50

SAMSON THE HOUSECAT 50

WHITE GUARDIST POETESS 51

Attempt at a Room 52

Her Dislove of Love 54

The Heart Ghost 55

Days in Red Poland 56

So Warsaw's Come to Wait on Us Now 57

Antipersonnel Mine 60

Skirt of a Thousand Triangles 63

Notice 65

District Behind the Lines 67

Black Re-partition 68

Rowe's Fawn 70

Honeycross 71

At the Hand and Pen 73

Telltale 74

The Makeover 75

My Angelism 76

The Barns of Joseph 77

The Goddess of Smallpox 78

House Private 80

After Afterlude 82

Butterfly Memory Object 83

Black Stone Mantelpiece with Chimney Clock 84

The Chess Queen 86

Who Is Your City? 87

FOR THE JADE-MAIDENS,

RUTH, MABEL AND ROSEMARY

*In 1797 four young militiamen were tried by Court Martial
in Belfast for connexion with the United Irishmen, convicted,
and immediately afterwards shot at a place called Blaris or Blaris
Moor in the County Down, near Lisburn; in an event that caused
intense and widespread indignation in Ulster. To commemorate
this, a spirited ballad of eight verses—of the characteristic
peasant type—was composed, the author of which was believed
to be Garland the 'Lurgan Poet'.... That the ballad should have
been sung to so many different airs and settings, in Munster
as well as in Ulster, indicates its widespread popularity.*

P W JOYCE
Old Folk Music and Songs, 1909

BLARIS MOOR

AN EARLY APOCALYPSE

I see the skeleton of the year
poised in the cool moonspray,
trying to catch at the blemished
calendar of the next.

Embraced most of the day
by the low and slender rainbow,
the world-jewel sweeps on
with its morning, noon and night.

The nowhereness of the fifth-month grass
stayed for a moment only,
before the earthless mountain light
anointed without mountains.

THE READING FEVER

The heart experiences systole,
small controlled doses of forgetfulness.
The intellect performs a full resolution
as though to a light by which
it went on being touched
on the continent's northern fringe.

The world is like a ring from a spouse
not yet stabilized in glory,
a sacrament performed by an unworthy priest
whose superessential gleam is hidden
in an offering—the sensible, the coastal
grasses still in winter head, the apple.

THE NYMPH HAY

If the muse should choose a language
she would choose this flawless English
to fold her thought in that entire quasi-family
of words, as I filled the false pockets of your coat
with uncombed lavender blossoms.

Once familiar things are more naked
than your skin darkened with *soorma*,
a Russian word meaning destruction,
as in the first wartime colour photograph,
Zenana, true bed woman, Saint Quadphone.

THE STONE-WORD

A finer-grained time lies thicker on the ground.
We take out the warm lining of overcoats,
replace one sleeve with a sleeve of a different colour.

Beyond the slower times the city dreams itself,
dreams *of* itself, its footprints, the nightwalk,
alarm all night becomes a kind of weather.

There was no walk, not for me, nothing to read,
sick without books, I wasted day,
the young, strong, demanding sun, the unwounded leaves.

Useless in the shadows of the sheds, I invented
a small abandoned notebook of doubts
concerning words, held it between my two heart fingers.

And the sight of the end of the platform
loosened a very long perfume that had ease
of gathering into my ceiling blue as an eyelid.

TRANS—SHIPMENT STATION

A cloud of down feathers hovers
about the city
like the nakedness of the right hand
touching the left.

Two letters on weather,
patterned in the form of kisses,
ushered in a moonlight that scalds
the shell-pocked Holiday Inn.

Someone agreeing to a kiss after death
is trying to stand up where mothers
taught their children to fall to the ground.

An acute memory of two kisses
situated between two other kisses
made a trench in my forehead.
Dustings of mud disintegrated
on the bed.

If a mountain is to appear
when we are willingly considering war
of an evening he slowly raises
his open hand and holds it above his eyebrows,
light blue being the infantry colour.

MUSK

With moorlike beauty the moon
that served in the autumn as a lamp
reappears and seems the one living
deserving thing already above
the horizon for much of the night.

The year is complete: each season has set
its sharp stamp on the land.
And after the easiest winter of the war
some of us who overlapped for six years
are born into that sanctuary, the lean spring.

The floor of last year's ragged tent
is carpeted with reindeer moss and cranberry
blossoms, as if a heart, on whose shoulder
my tent was placed, had burst through
its sleeping skin, from the weight of the snow dome.

Snow-beaten, the snow floor of the double igloo
feels like rice. No scab of ice
forms on our weather-ravaged faces
as dawn greys the burning dry-ice window.
Snow falls thinly, and I can imagine them

crossing the empty white sea
in other winters, the long frosted feathers
worked into their rain clothing
like Egyptian eyes on a dress
always frozen in its vision.

His hand always warmer than my own,
his broad, peaceful arms bringing
two miracles into being at once,
with one knee pulled upward he anchors
his sled with a flourish and birdlike amen.

His name-soul has cried herself
completely dry, and offers her half-moon breast
for a flat-tongued kiss, which touches them
into words, a voiceless *L*.

The consonant is drawn out tenderly
as snow snakes and patches their fireplace
of three stones, which makes

the soot-greyed icicled walls in which
they stand a fictive chapel,
awkward, urgent as a photograph,
while the ground-wind dies
painlessly, under the shallow snow.

ANIMALS OF THE MIND

Carrying bee bread, a healing
exudate from wounded plants,
the western honey bee in morning lows
passes through small flight holes
around each hanging combsheet
to a deeper part of the hive.

The crocodile, basking in the sun,
with jaws open, swallows stones,
but not the crocodile-bird spinning near.
A kneeling stag with distorted antlers
dies behind a friendly thornbush,
a lioness crouches among bronze leaves.

To be gifts, a border of walking lions
looks straight ahead in a guardian pose.
A gold and lapis lazuli ram is caught
on a tree where tiny silver frogs
play with lion pins. A team of four overlapping
yellow-glazed horses paws the raw evenings.

A camel with translucent eyelids
breathes the dead airspace next its skin,
exhaled veins returning to the heart.

A leaf is arrayed across the face
of a leaf-nosed bat, or nose-leaf bat,
the notch-eared, long-fingered, tomb or horseshoe bat.

When the moon dives, the moonfish, pufferfish,
spade fish, triggerfish and the upside down
catfish run after her like puppies.
Then a living blizzard of birds overflies:
the rose finch, shining sunbird,
the brown fish owl and the red-eyed dove,

the spectacled, Orphean warbler,
the mourning wheatear and the laughing thrush,
the dusky eyebrowed thrush, the rubythroat,
the slaty-headed parakeet, the sooty gull,
the plaintive cuckoo, the harlequin quail,
the see-see partridge and the ruddy shelduck;

the honey buzzard, the dark chanting goshawk,
the comb duck, the cotton pygmy goose,
the bean goose, the common goldeneye,
the shy albatross, the sociable lapwing,
the whale-headed stork, not the false killer whale,
the pond heron, the Indian blue robin . . .

Their airy eddies scatter juniper
for six miles of tongue-patterned serpents,

and Isabella gazelles, and marbled polecats,
and monk seals and harbour porpoises,
and naked-soled gerbils, and midday gerbils,
and click beetles and jewel beetles;

for the black-lipped pika and the white-toothed shrew,
for the junglefowl, the hinny or mule,
for the plain tiger butterfly and the mouse-like dormouse,
and the daughter the snake obtained by prayer
that was killed by a falling star, around the eye,
partly by the sure-lined way she holds her body,
partly by the ribbing on the wings she has acquired.

THE CONTENTS OF
THE CUPBOARD

When she goes to the Paragon
someone stands treat, you know.
Her splendid salary of four shillings
is subject to deduction in the shape
of fines—a fine of three pence
if her feet are dirty, or the ground
under the bench is left untidy.

A fine is inflicted for talking,
if a girl is late she is shut out
for half the day, that is for the six
morning hours, and fourpence
is deducted from her day's eightpence.
One girl was fined a shilling
for letting the web twist round
a machine to save her fingers being cut.

To contribute to the statue the foreman
stopped one shilling each out of their wages,
and further deprived them of half a day's work
by closing the factory, giving them a 'holiday'.

The husband can hear of no work
but evidently owing to bad temper
cannot keep a situation long.
The room has practically no furniture
except the bed, and when he has a fit on
he would not think twice of lifting it
and throwing it out of the window.

The baby is small, there is an old box
which does duty for a table. At the first visit
I got the husband to get a pennyworth
of coal, make up the fire, and wash the basin
they washed in for mixing the pudding in.
They were astonished that a suet pudding
could be so light, had never heard
of baking powder being used.

The mother stores milk in a jamjar
on the outside window ledge with a piece
of glass on top. The drinking water
is fetched up from the yard in a kettle.
The contents of the cupboard
have been noted down, as follows:

Lowest compartment—coals, splintered wood,
old newspapers, boots, potatoes, onions,
a stray carrot, and one or two cabbage leaves.

First shelf from the bottom—a frying pan,
back to the wall, cold pickles or jamjars,
empty tins, a paper of tin-tacks,
a penny bottle of ink (no cork),
a penny tin of vaseline (no lid),
a piece of soap, an old hairbrush and comb,
a few bent hairpins, bits of string,
a screwdriver and other tools,
a book or two, a magazine.

Second shelf from the bottom—a plate
with meatbones, cold potatoes and bacon rinds,
a bottle of vinegar, a biscuit tin
with the King in scarlet uniform,
a paper of tea inside, a brown teapot,
white and gold cups and saucers (incomplete),
a blue glass sugar bowl with brown sugar,
condensed milk in an opened tin,
a yellow jug, several spoons, forks
and knives in various stages of use,
round tin trays, some loose jam
in a pie dish, some pickled red cabbage,
a reel of thread with a needle stuck in it,
a battered thimble, a box of baby powder
with a puff in it, some safety pins,
a paper of flower seeds and a little blue bag.

Top shelf—a bundle of old papers,
more tins, bottles, jars and pots,
an old black shawl rolled up,
an old black sailor hat standing
on its side, with hatpins in it,
a broken birdcage, a saucepan with a hole
in it, stuffed out of the way.

TAVOLETTA

Before the snow of the city
too soon after Christmas
had three times melted
under the tenderest sewing clouds

all that was audible
was the last island in motion
cascading like a slanting plate
or a discarded crinoline

in the buckled roof of the rain.
The mind does not know
it is counting caustic sands
rushed from solid rock.

The picture hanging over my stove
gradually deepens its bone brown
to a holding back of colour without end
such as prevails at dawn

to older colours where rose
bleaches out and blue suffers.
Dark violet bricks in feathers
on the weather side of a wall:

an airwell on the left wing—
golden crucifixion through which he slept—
which is enough protection in itself,
but emptier than the parish church.

THE RAINBOW DIVISION

There does not seem to be any reason
why the hills should go where they do:
the land crouches like a badly broken
loaf of bread, the spoon-shaped ground
pretty as an English park
with larkspur and mustard flowers.

A corner of Thrace. Across the Hellespont
a high, straggling cliff upshoulders
white tents spread under sheltering
plane trees. Whirling windmills
crown the crest
of the ridge of Gallipoli.

Bullock carts with ungreased wheels
toil across Kodja Chai bridge.
Clean cattle with heads bent low
pull rectangular ammunition boxes,
black water buffaloes
drag flour bags, kneeling camels

untangle their necks and limbs
to prop themselves and begin

their side-wheel march.
It is not lack of rifles that worries
General Liman von Sanders
as he rides along the trenches

from the Dardanelles to the Aegean.
In the bar of the Salonika Hotel
a squad of German marines drink
Constantinople beer and sing
Fatherland songs:
the *Majestic* was sunk at daylight,

shaking the Sea of Marmara
with a deep prolonged roar
where an officer takes an inventory now
of the wrecked submarine.
Here and there, drab soldiers
straighten out short lengths of barbed wire—

the Turkish kind is oversharp
and thick as your little finger.
Brown-barrelled guns point south-west
where time and again I turn back
to the grey hulk forsaken
on the water. Two thousand

shells per hour fell, the battleships
splashing high fountains
till the mosque at Chanak was a ruin.
Before me cranes swing outward
and inward, a destroyer with a dark green band
flies the French flag astern.

A seaplane circles over.
The turbanned chaplain gazes past
the Red Crescent Hospital
to the plains of Troy and the hills
of Ilium, where Argive Helen
saw the brass-clad Greeks arrive

in their beaked boats. A giant
yellow balloon directs the gunfire,
and only the wounded under a rain
of copper-coated lead leave
these oddly shrinking, shell-swept
shores. And it so happened

that a fog came on, in the afternoon
the bush caught fire, forcing the troops
to move in single file
along goat tracks through the scrub.
Some strayed in search of water,
some pricked holes in the hoses with their knives.

On Hill 10 they had no artillery,
no stores, on C Beach only one
Field Ambulance. A commanding officer,
sixteen officers, and two-hundred-and-fifty
men charged into the forest,
were lost to sight or sound,

and never seen again. Many
were frozen to death as they stood,
the earth below the hospitals became infected,
before the season of the south winds,
mourning cards were sent, lamenting all five sons.

HOW DESPAIR MAY BE TRANSFORMED INTO A DIAMOND

As payment for your colour storm
an acid sky blackens every flower.
You feel your breath touching down
and hold on to the voice you know
on each lip corner, two now frozen
hedges to your country.

You can still alight on words
or sharpen them as you wish;
you can linger and stretch them
like the skin of a birch-bark letter
read before a mirror.
How easily you get what you want!

But if you step on the spot
the fully grown mouth passes
the feather of a red-headed
Irish angel three times between you.
When you are breath-bound
it is purely breath that is stopped.

THE MIGRATION OF
THE NOBLES, 1603

Alas, the heart that devised—
alas, the mind that considered—
alas, the speech that adjudged the advice
through which that party went on that journey.

The roads were not royal roads
though daisy-covered and clover-flowered.
In a highly indulged church (no woman
ever enters by its door)

they were shown a fourth part
of the body of St George, a shoulder
of St Laurence, a tooth of Peter's,
the forefinger of Thomas the Apostle,

the chalice out of which
John of the Bosom drank, one of the Thirty
Talents, two of the thorns, the column
of red marble from which the cock crew.

They saw also the trenches
at the river Somme
taken by three Irish companies.
There will be bitter outcries

when the corpse comes thither
at the behest of the left-handed angel.
A pity not to have Dundalk
instead of Louvain outside,

and the Cashel family on the street
instead of men who speak Dutch:
a pity that it was not young Maighréad
who was good wife in this house

last night. A pity
it is not Richard Óg
who comes with a bright cup
to O'Neill's table.

BY THE ENTRAILS OF CHRIST

The O'Neill, or Tiron, born in Dungannon,
reared in Dundalk, despite his Pale upbringing,
addicted to Popery, spent most of 1602
on a *crannóg* in South Derry, outside Desertmartin.

The ship was a Frenchman and came out of Brittany,
sailing from Dunkirk, but letters brought she none
from the King of Spain or Archduke. They should remain
beyond seas upon the King's charge,

leaving their horses on the shore with none to hold,
after the manner of the Tartars, where they best
like their pastures. He carried the sacred vessels
of Armagh to the friars of Flanders,

being met at the Ponte Milvio by the said Archbishop,
with eight coaches and six horses to each.
They worshipped at the seven privileged altars,
the Earl and his gang, they walk even now these streets,

in black weeds, after the fashion of grandees,
rapid-marching flambeaux of waxlights.

VIRGINIA WILL
BECOME AUGHANURE

Wood-famine bends my shiring maps.
Only the moon's full sleepwalking face
swelling out the walls seems fully alive,
faded indigo its standard of intangibility.

Yellow leaves lie fossilled in the roadway
where all market cries have been forbidden:
the crested lark and the Calandra lark
build lucrative niches on the bark of trees.

Each time we forded the baser river
a freshness rose from the fineness of the water,
the veins of sand. Unangeled now and colourless,
the still very bloated lough

stretching the old rounded image of the island.
The blue gorse sliced its view
into tree-abounding land parcels
whose branches pressed like moths

that filled each wasted county like a sack.

PRIMROSE RED ORCHESTRA

A glorious thrush has been singing on the mount
in peak foliage ever since daybreak. It has sung
three sounds of increase, while fifty years
has passed for each, back to the duelling cathedrals,
back to the physic garden, to the remains
of a small kneeling weeper
by the unringed cross with hollow armpits.

There are five fireplaces, one above the other,
straight up the wall of the dim-remembered war.
None with his goodwill will be called
Henry, Edward, Richard, George, Francis,
but rather Murrough, Moriertagh, Turlough,
suchlike harsh names. Your way
of working out Easter will be an English surname
of a town, as Sutton, Chester, Trim,
Skryne, Cork, Kinsale, a colour as white,
lotus white, toga white, black, brown,
art or science, as smith, or carpenter,
office, as cooke, or butler.

Accurate as the multiseasonal rose,
or a kiss that is led up to the white
eyes of the dead, only inches from women's

faces, only minutes, I walked along
the flint shaped island as along
the half mile of Easy Red, the first wave,

to find some graves with shears,
the gems of the household, sandglass
measuring the length of a sermon
and four-hour watches, *Meles meles*,
the complete skeleton of a dog in a sack,
the chestnut breast of the merganser.

That moment, when the sky was darker
than the water, a tiny probe had landed
after the furthest fall, on the frozen surface
of the only moon that has an atmosphere:
its heatshield worked perfectly, its three parachutes
opened as planned. And now it is like looking
with the Earth's original eyes
at the primitive, hallowed earth of monastery.

SANTO SPIRITO
LANDS ON MARS

Looking at the picture seems almost a form of trespass:
it would never have shown itself as it did,
this finely chiselled scene, a red, cobbled road,
rust-red tiles that shiver in ordinary sunrays.

It is somehow toylike, the light that plays
is unashamed like the light after heavy rain:
stark rocks in a bay, shell-headed,
terracotta roundels to be held in the palm,

all carved from the softest *pietra serena*,
a metalwork collage, a scattered bombardment,
the plainest of stone in a great stone chorus,
a kind of stone bouquet high in the air.

Mistily distant, they might still be moving,
on their seismic way to somewhere else,
they might be only sinking into the ground
like the piecemeal stones of a city,

an image of Florence, another Athens
or a second Rome: a mosaic
of tanned memories, shadows of Byzantium,
craggy and barren view of the afterlife

whose infinite space has been bound here
into a nutshell, a weathered floor
where we might find it easier to walk
in the radiance of another planet's days.

WHITE CORTINA OUTSIDE
STARDUST BALLROOM

I was seventeen years when I lost
my country and my girlish single
braid. They were completely new
days, the air above the brutalized
city was naturally trapped, dead silver
flecked with a germ-soaked beauty.

The sky under a rainbow
is lighter than the sky above it,
the way light is bent inside raindrops.
The sky between a double rainbow
is darker, the dark band
is caused by sunlight bent upwards,

a bright blue rag colour for dyeing
yarn, for glaze over silver, letters
in blue. Variations in the colour
of the sea, and longer into spring
than seemed bearable, the sky slowly
sipped away to willow ashes.

It seemed to have, I would like to say,
hands, though they were not seen,
those breathless ghosts of mine.
All cherries had taken their farewell
of their perfect cherry colour.
I could feel everyone praying for me

like a little forest bird,
the otherest. My light shone
on frost-shadows, rose-pink
on the hand, like down, such
as that of the vulture. A thick layer
of fragrances comforts the brain

and memory. I was being
distilled or simplified, like
a westernizing eye-shape. Our only
tree in more costly storms
fell into my dream's pale field
as water that will part gold

from silver, or our grace from
lack of it. Winter takes me
deep again to where she was
already root, the death
of my dream of how to paint
wounds, with the art that hushes.

THE STATEMENT OF MY
RIGHT HONOURABLE FRIEND

The me-ring that you buy yourself—
I want to buy a blood-bright gown
and let into its collar the satin
you gave me as a hood

which makes me think of you, day
and night. The wind is wrapped
in the longish grass, it shoots
the constant arrow of its voice

so all the time you are looking,
looking, at a moon possessed
by its planned dreaming. I cannot say
how sooner or later it must start,

it does start, in those parts of town
that mock their own seediness.
I am no longer standing in the coal
lorry, telling people anything.

I am under it, I am either under
the vehicle beside the wheel,

or behind it, beside the wheel,
my view has now dramatically altered.

I remember saying, do not run—
you say that you noticed two bullet cases
on the ground near the Saracen,
and they were split wide open

like flowers, spent, yes.
Because of the way they were open,
they were almost like daffodils—
everyone was saying that day

that if they spread like daffodils,
they were supposed to be dumb—
I know nothing about anything like that.
A Knight of Malta came to assist.

He was half-down, shaking, putting his hand
out in front of him, you know,
not fully up, crouching down, that was the way
he walked, hand out, with a handkerchief in it.

I had only a mental view, I saw nothing,
nothing is perfect in this world of riots,
there are always gawpers, hooligans, I am afraid,
on the edge of a riot.

From seventeen minutes past four,
you must have been there, Soldier S,
as we have to call you. Are you saying
something that was put into your mouth?
We can't have that now,
can we, Private?

Things may have been altered to suit
things at the time. Can I just,
will you bear with me a moment?
If people want to have a conversation

will they please go outside, at once?
If you have noticed I have not relied
on a memory that does not exist.
You do not have a memory,

do you, do you? If you say so,
yes. No, you have said so.
I follow, it is not correct,
but I follow, yes.

THE QUESTIONING
OF SOLDIER L

This month is called a tender one:
it has proved so to me but not
in me. I have not uttered one folly,
the more for the softness of the season.

In cloudy networks we may all
be netted together by darksome affections.
Disquietful, we lived and lived
strange moonscenes, a consider-the-lilies attitude.

Bubble-blowing Caprice with a weathervane
on her helmet, unless I see her life
branching into mine, she gives me no
ancestral help, elegant curve of fear and faith

whose arrangements of eggshells
had the ghosts of poems in them,
knowing to call back, to listen to
electric speech when the call is lost.

As Mary's veil was said to become
luminous during night vigils, I love

internal greenness, rusty back ferns,
petals backed with pale violet.

You are asking a woman of a great
many words to recall half a dozen.
You expect me to believe you now,
I believed you then.

Me and my rhetoric should be some
where, inside my head my own
voice without any connection
to my mouth, in the feminized tea shop,

in the humming room. I saw nothing
in the hands of the man who fell.
They saw a rare and previously
protected thing, Mr Whoever Turns Up.

NOTE FOR BLIND

THERAPISTS

No one knows where the winter food
is coming from. My icons and their
night light set in a recognizable
island are so paralyzingly holy
they lack the reality of reality
as our green wallpaper coloured
with arsenic of copper has adopted
some ideal white, so sweet and conscious.

A forever Marybud of which I am less sure,
in my servility to dominant interests,
text-worker, state writer, sapiential
woman with my quasi-brand name
lending my voice to others' words
like Ovid's Echo, who can repeat,
but not originate, speech, the depth
of dark beneath which lies our day.

I had been living so far from words
in my former wordlessness that to speak
often seems a kind of police work,
ventriloquizing the words of another.

I had been mapping the world for so long
through Hiberno-English, a hair's breadth
departure from a crust of dead English
to the unsayable void of the Portadownians.

A silent receptacle of many echoes
so overrun, and skimmed for the scant
cream of sense, or any sediment present
to my own available vocabulary
being spoken through, damozen, lap summer
skirt, rendered blue in the face
by the sonnet form, that liberates
the thousand river names from their anchorage.

I bescribble and I blacken paper
with my smooth domesticated tissue
of images desiring to please a shadow,
to saddle with meanings the traumas of war
by an occasion of wordshed.
Language deserts the self
like the fragility of the outer meaning
playing on the joy in Joyce.

A pillow of old words with old
credentials, never certain that their
passports are quite in order,
nothing with which to express,

nothing from which, no power,
no desire, with the obligation
to find semantic succour, and no
audience—that's part of one's death.

A NOVEL ABOUT PATRICK

Second or third house on the left coming up,
second floor, window twenty-one, I believe.
Window looking for a window, the window
at your back, sitting on the window-sill,
watching the opposite pavement thick from strain.

As you read, try the word on, kingly plunderer,
to be found stolen in a century. You should stop
using these minimum dreams as fuel,
I so enthustiastically underscore lines of yours,
I haven't been to the pawnshop in two months.

And right you are, never is, never was,
you just listen, listen—you hit the nail
on the head, you were as good as here, and burst
in you will, as if the presence of a faultless angel:
how two-in-one you are to me,

my soul is not that virgin. So he went on promising,
(page torn) and this over and over, she was crying,
she was undressed by a man with your ring on his hand.
At the city limits she watched eighteen trains go by,
her eyes cannot be paired up, sodden doorways of flame.

I am weary of cranial partitions and fabulously busy
like giving birth for the twelfth time and,
as fate would have it, I have so far been unable
to take my place at that window:
you force yourself through solid crowds

on pilgrimages buying in closed shops, your pocket
swelling with what was left over from the selling
of a medal, pocket lined with smashed eggs
and sunflower seeds. Please don't think I have designs
on the days of the week, like verbs with holes in them.

The past is ripped off like a shutter in a storm,
a car cries out like a cuckoo, or coughs
like an old man opening desk drawers. Once
the sirens sound I hold on to the edge of my Remington
from early in the morning, gun salvos broke

into our house at any time of the evening.
I was that angel of modesty that heated your flat
with my Greek scent, I would scrupulously
scrape my feet and clean my clothes with a brush
moistened in disinfectant. I opened

the storm windows to air I had ceased breathing
long ago, when I made that gesture of denial

against your hands, with the waiter standing
observing my mouth. New waves of the old feeling.
When the train came to a halt near the porcelain factory

they said there was a storm on the lake, they said there
was no storm. In a photograph I study with the eyes
of two families, the city rises outside
the windows of the Hotel Octobre,
my book smiles at me anew, from the window.

READING BEFORE STALIN

Friend means action—could you? Hold out?
In the northern capital we were not expected to know
what millennium it was outside Pegasus Stall
in that inconceivable London.

My lips cling together at the top of my voice
like fingers in mittens. As appetizers, cold slices
of marinated mushrooms, then mushroom soup,
and finally the main course, boiled mushrooms
with mushroom fillings.

My party books are dished out as dessert in little
cardboard squares, lilac ice-cream, cloud milk,
wine on the palm, cloud bread and rye-bread book.

The bronze of a sermon through the laziness
of the angels is melted down to a flywheel
with hammers, screws and bolts on a red
marble coffin. I can't get my hand

into my sleeve, what with the wooden spoon
in my buttonhole, the bluebird on my cheek,
the words across the sky displaying the day's motto,
a lyrical digression giving orders to the Army
of the Arts from the Commissar of Enlightenment.

VERSES UNPUBLISHED IN THE POET'S LIFETIME

WORKS AND DAYS

Although the blessing of horses
to Saint Florus and Saint Laurus
promised something, a stretch, from the road,
the calico balloon met the sky like John the Baptist—
above one's head hung not the spring.

OUR DAYS

The tulips became shorter and more abrupt,
the hill had grown taller and drawn in;
books that snaked across the floor vapoured
with the terseness of parable,
engines pounded hotly.

ABOUT THAT

Knives and forks on the terrace took on
a green hue, gatherings *à quatre*
made their nests high over the gangway
into a voyage on the round nape of the wave
just a station up the line.

SEASONAL MOOD PICTURE

Down by Brest Station the redolent express
departed into golden marshland and hillside
nurtured in silver—journeys became possible
to diamond forests, the river too
learned what it was to be renamed.

SKETCHES FOR A FANTASY

To put it more gently, I shall work my way
through to him, I shall break myself
for the last time, bewilderedly retracing
my steps and indried thoughts
like a hundred blinding photographs.

POEM OF A KINSMAN

I understood him as an outline, a contour,
a cast-off skin whose bandages would slacken,
whose youth was marked
by the dawning town that too often
became different, or nothing.

SYMPATHY FOR THE TWILIGHT

His alter ego, You Will Remain,
hid behind the claret-coloured walls of the cool
and clean museum. Farewell to loving
anything, I carried him away with me
from the boulevard into my life.

MUSE OF CINEMA

It was the middle sister who was the main
object of his interest—that was how
he operated—charred pears at the Café Grec,
her five-petalled gaze an ornate lock,
and little in the way of extra snow.

THE BLACK GOBLET

He finally seduces her, and in that instant falls
genuinely in love with her. Then
his mistress Camilla turns up
like a blood-spotted card.
(She lives next to the theatre.)

DREAM OF A FIRST LOVE'S MARRIAGE

He privately dedicated his sultry, summery
collection to Natasha, but she did not keep
his letters, and after his death her letters
to him were handed back to her.
(She has herself since died.)

REVENGE AGAINST MUSIC

He came from the depths of lyrical space,
alias the summer on the one hand,
to this mustering point, this profusion of lilac lustre,
this home in the autumn borne along
on its own words as though upon a raft.

YOUR DEATH

And the town that is now performing itself,
since she had replaced the whole blackened town,
stone by stone, surrounded by fir saplings,
whoever you are, this town is your own invention,
and what, the duty of something unthinkable, went on there.

SYNAGOGUE WEDDING

A tank cleared up the street like a forest cutting
once and for all, the drawing room over three winters
merged into one, was allowed to freeze up,
with venomous courtesy the first government decrees
made them remove their hats.

RED CORNFIELD

Everything disposed one to work, polite
social occasions were so few. The skittish
mannerisms of his backbone flute were unpolished,
like oars at rest. Still to him a schoolgirl,
she intended signing on as a nurse.

RAIN-SPANGLED POEM

And she was as good as her word.
They paid her in gold to pass through this atmosphere
of fierce, abstracted, chaotic frost,
of dirty sea and narrow beach by the rail
halt on the winter mail route.

TO THE DEMON'S MEMORY

But still mountains unlived by anyone.
Noise of a revving motorcycle flooded
the key buildings. October would be withdrawn
into even deeper depths, its frozen
motionless energy a puzzle to the two of them.

THE COURTYARD

I've appointed your meeting with me in a novel,
my brother in the fifth season of the year,
something more than a thousand pages long.
Having breathed its falsehoods for over ten years
I shall not manage this spring.

LYRE OF LYRES

Yesterday I began struggling through
the dense shrubbery of your book, your sweeping,
winged script, the aristocratic burr
of your French speech. But nor did I pour away
the ink with which I wrote of famine.

OCTOBER'S MAN OF THE MOMENT

Your book sounds its mating call, turns its ten
windmills in a huge wave of love. Splinters
of its lines fly apart and become caught
in ordinary drops—your voice is more mine
than yours, more aspen than birch.

UNEXTINGUISHED MOON

I stopped reading on the second page
where my family crystallized like stored water,
biographically glittering, deprived of Europe. Unshaken
by the changes down the street, all the elements
of the confusion are in him true.

SAMSON THE HOUSECAT

He is not the only one who can provide
a key to the age in his converse with the country,
its trading and careerisms, like a great mass
of time imagined all at once,
with faith in the reader.

WHITE GUARDIST POETESS

Simply as sharing the light of your *après-ski*
attention, to the soul in my soul, that rejoices
for the song that is over my song, comrade
genius, weary equestrienne, I snapped—Good!—
the book to on the third page.

ATTEMPT AT A ROOM

I had not counted on my letter's having not two
but four destinations, tight-lipped when pressed,
writing the poem about England for the newspapers.
I've not a soul to swipe an anthem from.

He always sounded bits of paleness in her universe,
his firmer mouth wandered, though hers was the heavier breath.
Some shred of heart the last vestiges of her mind
would not let go—I am as he is, since he is right.

His gait ringing on the steps, his bestowed weight—
despite his unerring ear all has been taken in advance,
he breathes on me the bitter cold of a possessor,
of whose possessions I am knowingly a part.

My warmth has already lain on the panes of his eternity,
there is always a sort of draught between you and me.
While speaking to a friend she hasn't seen for years,
oh, are the towels hung up to dry? What is ours

remains ours, I called it happiness, let it be misery
or the same aloneness. I had anticipated the entire
echo, would there ever be one to help us to fullness
again? Did I read you correctly, or just the movement

of your lips, should it be done with the eyes or with the breath?
Double jealousy—single is enough—our both referring
to the sea, the beginning, the northern city, dreary
and prosaic. You might have seemed to be made of an alloy,

on the assumption that you and I were translucent.
Remember, under coverlets of cowardice,
the birds on the ceiling and by the glimmer of memory,
the blizzards on the other side of the river?

Look at the map, the date, the town, out of the well
of wells the bed, back, table, elbow, always stove,
broom, money, none, not to sweep, any more—
the deed and the poem are on my side.

Though much, everything even, remains in the notebook.
Incomplete angel, either can speak for both,
we sit when we should stand, somewhat flushed,
in a secondhand bookshop.

And the blizzard of print increases in ferocity,
the long years are running out,
the gravely ill metaphors must eat their fill
before the hearse carries them to the churchyard.

HER DISLOVE OF LOVE

Women there are whose perfume
is ruinous and fine—they're thirty.
After the snarled tangle and cave-in
of the war my hands so seldom want to.

I took you to see your younger sister
beyond the suburb's brow: just anyone
who feels at home in the hours.
Journey of sacred slowness

to what you mean, my little word.
The woods are mine, pre-sounds
and post-sounds, where I can be
alone with your large photograph.

Last night I stepped out to take down laundry
and took all of the wind, all of the north, in my arms.

THE HEART GHOST

A dream stood over me
attracted by the lamplight
out of sight: a shredded face
that came back from the dead
of its own accord

to comfort the living.
Only its head was visible,
the shelves of brow and chin
as if preserved in redness like
a Prussian town now in Poland.

DAYS IN RED POLAND

Winter, without journey: I watch too much weather.
The slum clearance has turned old lush gardens to blood,
making noise like a bank in a blizzard
of constant views and surfaces.

From the unhealthy Jewish town within this image
of undamaged city I throw a can of pineapple juice
at a streetlight's unipolar world—a nested act,
with dragging slipper walk.

And move that sound aside like the earliest known word,
keeping guard over my ear all the time (my system just
has on and off) for cup-muted sounds that tend
to stop half way,

but looking for untasted words, though whispers
have their own key, and seeing everything as if it were
scenery. If I try to drink the paving waves
in the lavender-coloured mirrors,

or hold up the wall in my head with a third
hand, the dream ebbs out of me. I tie my Palestinian
scarf, stained teal-blue, ash and parchment
like that small 45 the Englishman wears.

SO WARSAW'S COME
TO WAIT ON US NOW

The war kept brewing. On and on.
We were rotting away. Who would
have thought it would last so long?

I wanted to escape to the Old Town.
I felt as if I were in some strange
German city crippled by the stones
under my feet.

I kept going in circles doing nothing.
I had so much to say, I preferred
not to be snared by words.

From early in the morning we heard
artillery and machine guns:
without that 'music' we were sad.

We received a spoonful of good jam.
At night we gathered snow.
The mass started at seven instead of midnight

because of the curfew.
I wanted to appear very devout
by walking the six kilometres to church.

Living in the country was the best
medicine, being put up at a new farmhouse
every twenty-four hours.

Zofia had a fall coat,
her place was a crooked shack sunk
into the earth as if for gnomes.

She perched on the packed dirt floor
like a hen, sealing herself with her shawl.
I took out our little pillow

which had lost half its feathers,
and next to it I folded over
many times my one and only dress.

Halina cut out a blouse for me
and some underwear from a pillowcase.
I sewed them up quickly.

We tried using our tongues
to wet each other's lips
with the fresh surface of water.

On the third day
we looked through our Lilliputian window
at a field of mute bricks.

Yes, he said, with his woven band
à la Tirol, this train belongs to me.
Armed with a pistol, with the safety off,

for the last time I fired a few shots
at the nouveau-riche smugglers
frequenting the coffee shops.

ANTIPERSONNEL MINE

Only 19-years-old, but I was called 'Father'
by a dying German soldier. He was old and fragile,
he did not have a weapon.
He lay twisted around his right leg
but when he saw the red crosses on my arms and helmet
his mouth stretched as if shrieks
were coming out, he reached for me
and cried 'Vater!'

I bared the wound at mid-thigh,
put sulfa powder on the exposed bone,
covered it with a compress, tied a loose
tourniquet. He was greying fast.
I stuck morphine in, he wasn't eased,
I gave him another eighth of a grain
and watched him lapse into shock.
I felt as if I too had been shot
and yearned to be dead.

*

Gordon got ripped by a machine gun
through the right waist. We were cut off
in foxholes by ourselves.
I tried to knock him out.

I took off his helmet, held his jaw up,
and whacked it as hard as I could.
I hit him with his helmet
but that didn't work. Nothing worked.
He slowly, slowly, froze.

*

I knew of shelters built inside
transformer housings covered
with metal-plated doors marked
with warning signs featuring
a skull and crossbones.
The people would drape
high-voltage cables over the iron doors,
in front of which they would place wet leads,
they were warm enough for someone to lie
on the floor even during sub-zero weather.

*

We don't have water. Everyone wants to drink.
People are simply burning up.
By chance I found a litre
while I was clearing away rubble.
Edka and I each had a little bit,
and then I took it back, practically full,
to our room for the others.
Lana came over—she is terribly thirsty.

I gave her the bottle and said,
'You drink first.' Marius came over.
Lana drank a third and asked him,
'Do you want a little water? Drink some and leave
some for Rena.' He drank
and put down the bottle.
There was not a drop left.

SKIRT OF A THOUSAND

TRIANGLES

It was minus 27. The city was drowning in flags.
We closed our still normal windows in order
not to hear the bells. All around the Market Place
enormous white poles had been planted
every one and a half metres, from which fluttered
bloody banners many metres long,
embroidered with a white circle. That same night
more than sixty persons were registered
as having committed suicide.

Having quickly sat down with my back
to the window I could only count the shots,
not the unravelled scarves. While I was binding
bandages, with my common-or-garden nerves,
she told me how precisely to knock upon the door
when a house was 'liberated'.
The first two days we spent
sitting on our suitcases.

When the porcelain isolators spaced at intervals
began to gleam white over the same forest-in-spring
she suddenly stopped addressing me as 'Sister'

and, looking desperately English, began kissing
both my hands alternately at high speed:
near perfume, the flowering
of my hands and fingers . . .

Her dress contains many skirts, one in-between skirt
of upside-down shapes, and geometrically
red endings—long, leafy, earthy ends.
At times she picks up to her northern shoulder
whole armfuls of her skirt to free her feet,
its soft, ladylike materials, its deceiving sash.

We exchanged a short, almost rough,
kiss on the march. You have to back out
of the cell as you leave, and tread on a rag
on the splintering floor, to draw the others
after you. To truly rebuild flowers of globe mallow,
hands outstretched towards the camp.

NOTICE

People selected for transport must leave their homes
in complete order. One piece of luggage
weighing sixty kilograms, and hand baggage
of a maximum of ten kilograms, will be allowed
per person. The remaining effects must be left
where they are in the home, e.g. curtains,
carpets, table lamps, wall mirrors, wash basins,
pieces of furniture, tablecloths, two towels,
and on the beds, mattress, bed linen,
and at least one pillow and bedcover,
all freshly made up.
Luggage must not be wrapped in carpets
or coverlets. If on inspection
it is observed that these instructions
have not been obeyed the person concerned
will not be taken on the transport
but will be sent to the interior to work.

The military has requested me to make it known
that under no circumstances may food supplies
be assembled among the local inhabitants
in order to deliver them to the prisoners of war.
Those who violate this command and nevertheless
try to circumvent this blockade

to allow something to come to the prisoners
place themselves in danger of being shot.
Special individual cases, contributions of near
relatives, will be negotiated through the commander.
I request you accordingly to make every effort
to stop possible collection and to explain
to the local inhabitants in suitable terms
about the facts of the matter—by order,

signed,

The President of the Government, May 1945.

DISTRICT BEHIND THE LINES

I carefully arranged the mask of buckram
curtains on my swan-pit features
like a blue-collar archangel who has turned
herself into a pet heron.

My father's old tied flat shorn of its partitions—
Mama reading, lamplit, sitting by the rose—
the necessary table set for six people—
a sip of two days' ago's tea:

fellow-traveller, the content may be ours
but the voice is theirs—'Northern Elegies'—
books interleaved with crumbled rice paper,
never-ending marks of uncomradely respect.

What difference in touch, white on green,
between the fur smell and the moss smell,
the flower value and the rose relaxed,
had you in mind? The hedge of clipped maple

as yet unringed with winter wreaths.

BLACK RE–PARTITION

The black bird that has been with me all my life
comes and sits on my shoulder and whets its beak
like a woman with perfume, always adding touches.
Touches of red, all stillborn.

I always had a set of dayclothes by my bed.
Our look is what kept the icy-cold pages unread.
Tie the petticoat tighter, as I was kissed yester e'en
by a man from whom pure spirit flashes from time to time:

taking a kiss outside time, a small fence of kisses.
Moon, bird and flower watcher, I picked out his rooftop
on the wrists of each day, all the rooms but one
without light, far more threatened than birds.

They call September the part in the hair, they call
the season ten, depending on how the joints
of the year are going. From a single family
of lightly travelled streets, from the guncotton

dried there, a second thread moon
in a sky of German blue falls on the elbow
of our opened river. *Is cuma liom.*

I walk impossibly uphill
with the collar hurting my decayed aura.
Our mothers thought by eights instead of tens.

ROWE'S FAWN

When Ireland was a cloud in the west
that could flex with the waves it was not
unknown for women to keep the Host
in their mouths in order to win a kiss:

falls of high-protein manna,
much of it gnaws at Ireland from afar.

Make of your left hand
not two triangles stitched together
but a throne for your right,

like the darnel—like the arm
of St Gertrude emerging from her shrine
to receive offerings.

HONEYCROSS

The clouds set immediately after the sun,
that merchant of astonishment, leaving the lower
branches scorched. The moon like the hand
of earth's clock, unlocked an innermost door
into a past garden.
                  Fifteen years ago, on Holy Thursday,
they left his corpse on a lonely road. The bloodier
newspapers showed the exact spot in his throat,
greyness of heaped paving stones, triangular danger-signal,
a confessional turned on its side, nicely exposing
his heart, red carnations dropped there.
                            I have more than once
ducked my head from the sound, it seemed incredible
that a woman was hanging linen up to dry
where rifles dipped their cranes in salute
like ill-groomed palm trees across the faded
vermilion roofs of the thickset city. Grandmother
back from the longer rigmarole of vespers.
Holy Trinity approaching, yet nowhere was there sign
of paint on shutters, weathered to a silver.

The earth was being pulled through some undrawn line
of rose-coloured farms and pearl-grey villages
to plants in their unhurried flow beneath the land,

standing on tiptoe: Christmas flowers that only seem
to live in moonlight, bruisewort, or common daisy,
the Warden pear, now our Black Worcester,
sweet woodruff for Corpus Christi, narcissi
which folk call 'Laus Tibi', rosemary, husband
of lavender, the seven spotted ladybird, Our Lady's
Bird, all guarded by Saint Dorothy of the Cherries,
a German garden saint.

AT THE HAND AND PEN

The large river the city does not have
but would be stopped by nothing flowed
towards the jail at the edge so everyone could
tell themselves, I went.

How many times had they closed the university,
shut down the lecture series? The horizons
had all been pleated like doubt-peacocks
shooed away. Like Fay,

cut in two by bombs, holding her little girl
low-breaking by the hand, or the ones shot
at crossroads. She sprinkled holy water
where the pavement was uneven.

He took his ballot out of his pocket,
raised it to his forehead, then traced
the sign of the cross with it over his chest
and placed it in the box.

TELLTALE

The city was covered as if by a spider's web.
To get to the centre one had to go past
at least fifty street sentries.
A simple trip required as much
as two hours through barricades,
checkpoints and tank traps.

A leg, its foot in a boot still attached,
a vast pool of dark blood
washed over the back of the market,
coursing around the cabbages, potatoes
and shopping bags. Cars doubled
as ambulances.

Pedestrian walkways were riddled with cavities
left by mortar and artillery strikes.
And after the war some were filled
as a telltale, with bright red plastic.

THE MAKEOVER

Four thousand acres of roses and carnations
leave the upgraded airport within hours
of being picked. The connectivity
of the most connected city is the television
sitting like an eyesore covered
with a global garment.

Private, non-world, three-speed city, to meet
and be seen, for whose beautification
perfume the colour of urine is sold
at traffic lights, whose vehicles slide
through vast excavations and monsoon-stains
for the under road flyover that will cut
the ring road's travel time.

On grilled balconies and languid seafronts
we sip Singapore Slings as though
the carnage had nothing to do with us.
The car he drove was so big it couldn't
come anywhere near where we live.

Everybody knows who killed him.
I know. If someone falls ill at night
there is a birdsong of mobile phones
in which I am always listening for her,
a serious girl who does not know her age.

MY ANGELISM

Our fifty-year-old linden trees
have put on another sign—
in smooth weather a blizzard
of red snowflakes, red cockerels.

In this landscape of untended woods
the oddly regular pattern
of young pines, flowerless
but trembling, bristles and turns

over a floor of field
where their trunks are drilled
into an avenue. The navy blue
police with their white armbands

without the number of life
square their fists off the outlawed
pavement. Sea stings the wall bearing
the mural and shallow-floods the rice.

The decayed sun closes its eyes,
a golden wash-beetle:
I'll praise the girl's slow looks
with the yellow of the gorse.

THE BARNS OF JOSEPH

Normalization: the square's new polished look,
the light as it passes between the buildings
moves parallel to the ground's honeyed marble
and fir-green mottling, finding themselves
on the street together. Sudden double red
of a cloud separates the losses to blue,
a second brown underlies the conceiving
black opening between the leaves.

This half-peace war is here
showing its peaceful face.
It has its front line of souls hovering
at knee-height in the indistinct dawn,
only two-thirds divine,
crozier-shaped wind heads.

THE GODDESS OF SMALLPOX

It's all-the-year-round Christmas
and, oh, come let Him adore you,
the astral linkings of the house
cooling, leaving the one superghost.

What with the magnificent art
of living, in the doubt of the extreme
game, the shroud of language
brings a silence full of certainty

pretending that language caused
the world—such an afternoon
world, poised between the crisis
of yesterday's sunset and the dying

snowflakes, festivals of the mind.
Death, they say, is not even winter,
a mere punctuation mark, as we listen
for her fragrance in the ice which her breath

has become. In some complete history
a universe might have these instant
meadows, might de-flesh or dress in new
bodies if dew in fact covered

both sides of their leaves.
But this slow-release enchantment,
from eternity's claustrophobic organic
spaces, must be God and his mental

events, his unconstrained imagination
and choice. Waking Him up
might make her vanish with her lime-
topped sword, her bedraggled peacock whisk.

HOUSE PRIVATE

Single rose,
simplicity,
single dahlia, treachery and instability.

The entire clothing used about the person
should be put into a tub of cold water
and kept outside the house for twenty-four hours.

Ladder fern, sincerity and sorrow,
holly, foresight,
ivy, attachment.

The house floors and woodwork
should be cleansed with hot water,
the walls limewashed, and every apartment
fumigated with chloride and vitriol.

Climbing roses,
unfailing love,
wild geranium, steadfast piety.

The personal clothes should be dried
before a strong fire, the bed,

if of straw, chaff, or shavings
as well as ticking, should be burned
within the yard attached to the house.

Periwinkle,
sweet memories,
unerring devotion.

Woollen articles should be cleaned
and exposed to strong dry heat.
A free current of fresh air
should pass through all the rooms.

Acacia, immortality.
Stephanotis,
will you accompany me to the East?

AFTER AFTERLUDE

The leather boats lift themselves
away from their ropes on easy hinges.
One passes the land of the dead
on the bus into town. One returns
from the root of the sky covered
in icicles. I focus on their glasslike
feel, their crystal breathturn.

What do you mean, I am rapid,
flying on breathways? No one
really dreams any more, the bread
of the dream, the haste of the dream,
yet anyone who awakes has overslept
the look of night, grass
written asunder.

My heart passes through the pause,
the whirring woods, the nettle message
of the ghetto-rose, that petalless flower.
I imagined God as a book, not
where you cannot be, eternalized,
non-eternal you, reader in the after
world, dropping your ghost-rosary.

BUTTERFLY MEMORY OBJECT

The simple outlines of tulips:
what makes these war flowers?
The war recycled like an earthrise
photographed from the distance
of a six-day-old moon.

The crags of their petals
dance out space with the smoothing action
of the mouth's own slidings
till their two-sided skin
bayonets the softer parts of shells.

Still deadly places are folded
into an unburial ground where resting
soldiers tell the munitionettes
they're easy to sleep with,
and for your button a kiss.

BLACK STONE MANTELPIECE
WITH CHIMNEY CLOCK

How much Sunday there was in the half-
discarded days—there and there, the flags
holding themselves ever more high,
stretching as if acclimatized
to the born landscape.

It had got too late for everything,
the lamp-yellow mirrors each contain
a different emptiness, smooth brown
in the eyes, the time of their first brilliance
sewn up like the sleeve stumps
of an armless man.

He makes his saints out of such things,
as if woven of fresh reed behind
this enduring: wide-open silver flowers,
hands that know how to sleep, that lie down
as if made of a single piece after all
that has passed, to rest for centuries
spread-open, starlike, dried flowers
as if in the wells of a paintbox.

With the lightness of a chime's voice
she gives her consent to the seasons,
all their violet hues tucked in, as it were,
like certain evenings, to this calm,
almost velvet-like air
which is surely not easily introduced.

Red orifice facing the front,
its inward carmine a little more yielding:
will one no longer have to carry
its heaviness? It was calling, as it had been
calling throughout the weeks, all the time,
it needed one in order to feel itself.

The things placed upon it add their comments
with all their heart, each in its own way,
but there is still some other object
on the bare mantel, pushed up
against the white cloth . . .

This way it is ghostly, it is still the same
heaviness place by place, the windows,
smaller than they were, reduced
and completely in the wrong,
of this self-willed old city, holding its own,
between right and left. Hilly, like light music.

THE CHESS QUEEN

Where a scar of sunlight leaks
some Eros for the dead
on to the low mist gap
in a haphazard afternoon
of errands that once existed,

a scarecrow with a yellow star
and silver flowers at her hips
gives the steadfast company
of affectionate immortality
to the dull world mood.

Someone is gone, someone
is sure to go, into the fruitful
afterlife of the ochre-coloured
twentyfirst-century water

newly cleansing over snowy
cobblestones old as the city.
The sound of the sun purifies
the spirits of erased aeroplanes
as long as they shimmer.

WHO IS YOUR CITY?

The canal's middle swells with waiting
for odd hours of night in the middle of the day.
North appears everywhere, the now of the snow,
warming ice counts itself away in different
sun angles, like a block of frozen ink
insisting on the line. The water knows
the way down, to the Titanic and her two
sisters. She rouges her silver likeness,
buttons her gown herself, so high, so closed,
her days malodorous from saturated skies.

Do you think it reflects well on our city
to ones who arrived only a week ago
to go outdoors in pyjamas to the turgid
bar district, the Gucci outlets in the city's
revamped living room? To photograph
a child on the King's Highway?
Arrival city—where disaster zones have become
more theatrical, ambitious parks obsessed
with self-esteem are honeycombed
with missions and endeavours and offers
of salvation as an incandescent life force.

Gone is the edginess of the city, cleansed
of conflict, argument, debate, protest, ructions
and ribaldry, notwithstanding the spy cameras,
the pop-up shops, the flash mobs of drink-
fuelled petrolheads, the new Purple Flag award.
I still have to define my life through the false prism
of Samson and Goliath, the ailing road perfuming
the heavy curtains of Parliament. We still show
our papers to reveal where we are going.

The street will no longer lie like a doormat
but plunge storeys down on to swift pavements
pedal-powered by driverless taxis. Nobody's
living there, nobody's moved in, it's sitting there
though the visitor centre is shut
and they are lifting the paddy fields on to the roof
which smells too much of museum dust
or pages from faded magazines. The waterfront within
the enabling bygone hedges is made of flesh.
I speak the language, I know how to be a woman here.

.